# US & British Virgin Islands Travel Guide

The Top 10 Highlights in US & British Virgin Islands

# Table of Contests

Introduction to US & British Virgin Islands...................6

1. Virgin Islands National Park ....................10
2. Charlotte Amalie .....................................13
3. Coral World Ocean Park .........................16
4. Magens Bay .............................................19
5. Buck Island Reef National Monument ...................21
6. Road Town ..............................................23
7. Mount Sage National Park .....................26
8. Anegada Island .......................................28
9. Norman Island ........................................30
10. The Baths National Park .......................32

# Introduction to US & British Virgin Islands

The Virgin Islands are a true border between the Atlantic Ocean and the Caribbean Sea. Politically speaking, this archipelago, which encompasses several islands, many of which are uninhabited, is divided into two territories: the US Virgin Islands and the British Virgin Islands.

The western islands form the US territory and it is comprised of Saint John, Saint Croix, Saint Thomas and Water Island. On the eastern area, the British territory has four islands: Tortola, Jost Van Dyke, Virgin Gorda, and Anegada. Each territory has many more small islands that are secluded.

The US Virgin Islands cover over 130.000 square miles of land and it has a little over 100.000 inhabitants. A true melting pot of different Caribbean and African culture, the area was originally inhabited by Caribs, Arawaks and Ciboney people. The islands were discovered by Christopher Columbus during the 15$^{th}$ century. In the next couple of centuries, several European powers occupied this territory, until, in 1672, the Danish West India Company took over the island of Saint Thomas. During the 18$^{th}$ century these islands became Danish territory and in just a few years they became a prime spot for sugar cane farms.

During the First World War, the United States of America, fearing that the archipelago might be taken over by the Germans, bought it from Denmark for the price of 25 million dollars in gold coins. By 1917, USA took possession of the territory which was renamed, from Danish West Indies the Virgin Islands of the United States of America.

All the while, the British Virgin Islands also had several European powers fighting over them after Columbus discovered them. Though the Dutch tried to establish settlements on the island of Tortola, during the 17$^{th}$ century the British managed to conquer the three main islands in the area: Tortola, Anegada and Virgin Gorda. Since then this archipelago was named the Virgin Islands, and only after the other islands became US territory, this archipelago was referred to as the British Virgin Islands.

Unlike its American counterpart, the British territory became a great hideout for pirates, particularly during the 16$^{th}$ century, when several European powers fought over these islands. During those times, the great legends of ruthless pirates like Blackbeard, also known as Edward Thatch, were born, and even to this day tourists in search for adventures come here in order to try and find metical treasures buried on the beautiful beaches of these islands.

Today the British Virgin Islands is just less than 60 square miles and it has about 28,000 inhabitants.

However the main attraction of both Virgin and British Islands are the dazzling beaches. Hundreds of miles of stretches of white sand welcome tourists any day of the year, thanks to their tropical climate and mild weather.

Snorkelers and scuba divers will also be in heaven here. Some of the greatest diving spots in the world are located on these islands, weather you are interested in the phenomenal barrier coral reef surrounding the islands of Anegada and Buck.

Sailing is one of the most beloved sports in the Virgin Islands, particularly on the British territory, and most ports are filled with shinny vessels. Large cruise ships also dock on the ports of Charlotte Amalie (the capital of the US Virgin Islands) and Road Town (the capital of the British territory). Here tourists get to experience the real Caribbean lifestyle with great restaurants and countless shops. In fact, Charlotte Amalie is sometimes known as the duty-free capital of the world, and many tourists love to indulge in some shopping therapy at one of the hundreds of shops here.

The British Virgin Islands boasts not only amazing pirate legends, but also unique places that attract thousands of visitors every year. The charming capital city of Road Town is a great place to start your exploration through these exotic islands. From there a visit to the Baths National Park is a must. Not every day you get to see such magnificent landscapes. The other lush natural reserves also are a great attraction for hikers and nature enthusiasts who want to spend their vacation in the wilderness.

All in all, the Virgin Islands are a perfect destination for any type of vacation, from beach bums, to fancy sailors, to adventure junkies.

# 1. Virgin Islands National Park

One of the most popular places in the entire Caribbean, the Virgin Islands National Park on the US island of Saint John boasts hundreds of plant species and interesting animals, making it one of the most breathtaking and gorgeous vacation spot for nature enthusiasts.

The park covers more than half of the island of Saint John and most of Hassel Island, encompassing over 14,000 acres of land filled with beautiful beaches, rolling green hills and coral reefs. The area also has a very long and interesting history. The first settlers lived here at the beginning of the 9th century and there are several remains of long lost cultures like the Taino people, including rock carvings, and petroglyphs. After Christopher Columbus discovered the islands, Saint John became one of the most important ports in the Caribbean and favorite destination for ships from all over the world. Soon after the land was discovered, the island quickly was populated with sugar cane farms.

Today, visitors exploring this national park can still see remains of that long history, including hundreds windmills, factories, great houses and warehouses that were part of several sugar cane farms. There are also thousands of old houses where enslaved workers used to live.

However, the main attraction of this park is its dazzling white sand beaches. The park is almost completely surrounded by the ocean and amazing coral reefs, making it a great destination for diving and snorkeling. There are several public beaches where most tourists [refer to spend their time, but if you are interested in more secluded places, there are plenty of isolated spots that look like a postcard.

Among the most popular places for sunbathing and swimming is Cinnamon Bay which boasts shallow clear waters and a wide beach. This is a perfect spot for snorkeling and wind surfing thanks to its low elevation. The bay is very close to another popular highlight – the Cinnamon Bay Plantation.

The most popular spot in Virgin Islands National Park is, without a doubt, Trunk Bay Beach. This long and arched stretch of sand is one of the most photographed places in the Virgin Islands and a perfect choice for tourists who want to spend a few days relaxing and basking in the gorgeous sun. Just like most beaches on the island of Saint John, here visitors can also discover the amazing underwater world where there are over 30 different fish species and a beautiful coral reef. This area is so beautiful, it was chosen by many prestigious travel magazines as one of the most beautiful place in the whole world.

However, this park is not just about sunbathing and snorkeling. The amazing biodiversity of the island is reason enough to visit the area. There are hundreds of plant species and dozens of bird species and the actual park has several marked trails, which lead by most plantation ruins. The most popular and beautiful trail is the one which lead to Bordeaux Mountain, the highest spot on the island. With an elevation of over 1,200 feet above the sea level, the mountain is the highest spot on Saint John. Those brave enough to finish the hike will be rewarded with some of the most impressive 360-degrees views over the entire park.

Despite the fact that this park is a very popular touristic destination, there are no hotels here, except for Caneel Bay resort, on the northern coast of the island, which used to be the famous American financier Laurance Rockefeller's personal estate. If you want to spend more time in nature you can choose from two camping grounds: Maho Bay and Cinnamon Bay.

# 2. Charlotte Amalie

Tourists with a penchant for pirate stories should not miss the opportunity to visit US Virgin Islands' capital city – Charlotte Amalie. Named after a Danish queen, this is the busiest port in the Caribbean, and a very popular touristic destination. Located on the island of Saint Thomas this port used to be a favorite among pirates thanks to its deep waters and secluded areas.

Nowadays the capital city has become a magnet for tourists in search for lavish beaches and great shopping and dining spots. In fact this city has the largest number of shops and boutiques in the entire region and it's no wonder why Charlotte Amalie is on the list of any major cruise ships.

The city is easily recognizable, even from afar thanks to its charming red roofed houses nestled between lush green hills. Once you step into city you'll find that most streets and buildings have Danish names.

However, the main attraction of the capital is the long and interesting stories of pirates and treasures. In fact, one of the most sought after places are Blackbeard's, which was built during the 17$^{th}$ century by Danish settlers. Blackbeard's Castle is a national landmark and it was originally built as a watch tower in order to protect the harbor. Though there's no actual proof that the infamous pirate Blackbeard actually conquered this castle, which, at the beginning was named Skytsborg Tower, but local legend says that Edward Teach, better known as Blackbeard used this tower to as a lookout for him and his crew.

The oldest standing building on the island of Saint Thomas is Fort Christian which today houses a museum with art and artefacts form the Danish period. The fort was built in 1680 by the Danes and throughout the years, it was expanded and had several purposes including a government building and a jail.

Another distinctive building in the capital city is the Legislature Building with its interesting green façade. This two stories estate was built during the 19th century and it was used as barracks for the Danish police. Today it houses the offices of the US Virgin Islands Legislature.

Charlotte Amalie is known for its narrow step streets which can be quite make otherwise simple strolls a workout. Nonetheless, a beloved spot in the city is the 99 Steps, a relic from the 18th century. In fact the staircase has 103 steps and is just one of the many that were built by the Danes throughout the city.

Charlotte Amalie is also a shopping heaven thanks to its duty-free policies. There are hundreds of shops and stores speeded throughout the city. Many tourists choose this destination mostly because of its endless shopping options rather than for its beautiful beaches. Not that this city doesn't boats several prime sunbathing snorkeling spots.

# 3. Coral World Ocean Park

Not too far from Charlotte Amalie, the Coral World Ocean Park invites its visitors to discover the amazing underwater universe. The Virgin Islands are surrounded by many incredible coral reefs, but many of them are endangered. This center strives to protect these precious ecosystems and also to educate tourists about their importance.

This interactive park boasts a 100 feet underwater observatory tower where visitors can take an up close look at the fascinating world undersea. Here, tourists can stay dry while admiring hundreds of fish and marine creature about 15 feet below the sea level. The tower has three levels. The top one offers great views over the coastline, and sometimes visitors can get lucky and spot humpback whales. The second one is also known as the Predator Tank and takes visitors through the world of sharks and other large fish usually found in deeper waters. The lowest level, Undersea Observatory, is the perfect spot to take in the entire underwater ecosystem, with amazing reefs, colorful fish, turtles and many other sea creatures freely swimming around.

Brave visitors can take their experience a step further and actually take a stroll on the ocean floor. The park offers visitors the opportunity to take a guided walk along an underwater trail. First visitors get a short training session, and then, with a specially designed helmet, that looks more like a space suit helmet, visitors are guided along a trail 20 feet underwater, alongside coral reefs and a wide variety of colorful and funny looking fishes. Those in luck will also get to spot turtles and even stingrays.

The Caribbean Reef Encounter is another beloved attraction of Coral World Ocean Park. Here, an 80,000 gallon tank houses a large coral reef. The top of the tank is open so that the natural elements can filter in and all the animals living in this ecosystem can receive natural light just like in the actual ocean. The unfiltered water allows sponges and corals to grow naturally giving visitors the chance to admire up close these amazing creatures. The tank also houses hundreds of colorful fish all of which are collected from the waters nearby.

Shark fans can admire these incredible creatures at the Shark Shallows which features several shark species. Those who are brave enough can even pet baby sharks, with the help of a staff member.

There are also several possibilities to come into contact with other sea creatures like sea anemones, sea stars, hermit crabs and other similar shallow-waters creature at the Touch Pool.

# 4. Magens Bay

One of the most sought after beach in Saint Thomas is the small stretch of sand at Magens Bay, located on the north part of the island. This is a very popular beach, not just for tourist but for locals as well. What is more, unlike most popular beaches on the island, this area is by the Atlantic Ocean, rather than Caribbean Sea.

Lined with beautiful palm trees and green hills, this less than a mile beach is a true paradise for any beach bum. The beautiful blue waters here are also quite shallow, which means Magens Bay is also a great place for diving, snorkeling, wins surfing and other water sports. However, snorkeler should not expect to find a wide variety of reefs and underwater species. Since this part of the ocean floor is mostly just sand, the only things of interest for divers and snorkelers would be the chance to see turtles, conchs and many fish species. However, the sandy bottom also means this area is perfect for swimming, even for beginners, since the waters are, usually, very calm.

The each is surrounded by some of the most beautiful natural areas, including an arboretum, a coconut grove and a mangrove. The area features several well marked trails which lead under tree canopies.

Right by Magens Bay, a five acres arboretum offers visitors the chance to explore the breath taking wilderness, including several rare tree species. The arboretum was established in the 20's and it was said to have contained hundreds of plant species, but throughout the years, the park was neglected and even destroyed by a hurricane. However, in the last decade, the arboretum was reopened and hundreds of new plants were introduced in the area.

Magens Bay is a great vacation spot for nature enthusiasts. The amazing trails leading through great natural wonders will certainly keep you busy for days and eve weeks. And, after a long day of walking and hiking, you get to cool off in the perfect blue waters of the ocean and relax on one of the most beautiful beaches in the world.

# 5. Buck Island Reef National Monument

Buck Island is one of the many small uninhabited islands in the US Virgin Islands, north of Saint Croix. The island was established a protected area in the 40's and the most important part of the island is actually underwater.

Buck Island attracts tens of thousands of visitors each year thanks to its over 4,500 acre long reef. This is truly an underwater paradise for divers and snorkelers who get to explore a large reef with all the sea creatures living there. There is even an underwater marked trail which leads divers along the elkhorn coral barrier reef. There are also several plaques with interesting facts about this amazing ecosystem.

Along these trails visitors will encounter countless tropical fish including barracudas, but also nurse sharks, lemon sharks, leatherback turtles, green turtles and spotted eagle rays. However, the best part is the infinite shapes, patterns, colors and textures of the coral – a true underwater fantasy world.

Though Buck Island's main attraction is its underwater treasure, the actual island boasts several idyllic beaches. The most beautiful one is Turtle Beach where visitors can relax and take in the amazing surrounding, after a day spent under the sea. Between the 30 feet tall barrier reef and the actual beach, the waters form a beautiful lagoon. From the beaches here you can admire a wonderful spectacle of colors once the sunlight reflects on the sandy floor.

The island also has several walking trails, great for a little over the sea level exploration, and many picnics sites. The hiking trails lead through ginormous tamarinds on a large ridge, from where tourists are treated with amazing views over this small island.

Buck Island should also be admired from afar. Though it is difficult to sail very close to the shore because of the barrier reef, several companies offer sailing tours of the surrounding area. There's no better way to admire this entire island than sailing around it while enjoying some rum punch.

# 6. Road Town

The capital of British Virgin Islands is one of the most popular cities in the area, with over 9,000 inhabitants. The city is named after the most important port on the island of Tortola, Road Bay.

This is the largest commercial center in the entire British territory with many shops and restaurants. The town features several old sugar mills and historic forts, many of them dating back over two centuries ago. Road Town is also a popular spot for yacht owners and cruise ships. The port is almost always populated with shinny vessels.

Though the city doesn't boasts the best beaches in the British territory, its charming small town feel is reason enough for a visit. Road Town can easily be explored by foot and that way you can take in the charming Caribbean atmosphere. You can explore every shop and boutique on the Waterfront, where tourists, usually, prefer to buy handmade jewelries, while the town's market is a truly melting pot for the islands' many cultural influences. Make sure you try at least one type of homemade jam! You won't be sorry!

Make sure you have a glass of true authentic rum which is distilled right here in the British Virgin Islands. There are several brands sold throughout the islands, but make sure you choose a local one, in order to experience the true taste of this intoxicating liquor.

What is more, Road Town not only offers many traditional restaurants, but several establishments offer truly British menus, including dishes rarely encountered outside the UK. The best restaurants can be found on the Main Street.

Not too far from the city, visitors can enjoy the amazing opportunity to swim with dolphins at the Dolphin Discovery. This park also offers several dolphins shows where curious visitors can see these amazing creatures performing tricks.

If you plan on staying more than a few days in Road Town, then you can even take a few sailing lessons. This is the city's favorite sport and the large number of yachts and boats docked in Road Port is a testament to that fact.

If you are interested in a more quiet vacation, the best way to take in the entire city is bay enjoying a refreshing rum based cocktail on a bench in Sir Olva Georges Square, right on Waterfront Drive. From here you can watch locals passing by and experience a fragment of this small city's daily life.

Despite the fact that it is the capital city of the British Virgin Islands, Road Town is a small city with quiet streets and not much of a night life. Compared with the neighboring Jost Van Dyke Island, known as the party island of the Caribbean, thanks to its large number of clubs and bars, Road Town is a peaceful alternative to the other busier islands.

# 7. Mount Sage National Park

Also on the island of Tortola, Mount Sage National Park is a large park surrounding a volcanic mountain. Mount Sage is over 1,700 feet tall and the entire park encompasses almost 100 acres of land, south-west of Road Town.

This is the first national park established in the British territory, after the land was bought from local farmers during the 60's. The park houses hundreds of plant species including old trees which cleverly hide a long ridge which runs from east to west through the island of Tortola.

Hikers and nature enthusiasts can spend days hiking through the thick forest all the while discovering the diverse ecosystem of the island. In fact there are twelve well marked trails, including a Mahogany Trail named after the founder of Mount Sage Park. All twelve of them form a circular route. The most beautiful parts of the park can be admired from Henry Adams Loop Trail, which also has several steps.

Sage Mountain is the highest point on both US and British Islands with an elevation of 1,716 feet. Those who manage to reach the peak will be rewarded with amazing views over the rest of de islands and part of the Caribbean region.

Locals say this national park has remained untouched since the first settlers arrived in the island. That is why this thick forest is populated by many bird species including hawks and hummingbirds, and hermit crabs.

With so many tropical trees and great overlooks, Mount Sage National Park is one of the best places for hiking in the Virgin Islands, where nature enthusiasts can explore untouched parts of this corner of the world.

# 8. Anegada Island

The second largest island on the British territory after Tortola, the island of Anegada is one of the most beloved spots among snorkelers, thanks to its impressive 18 mile long Horseshoe Reef, the fourth largest reef barrier in the world and the largest one in the Caribbean. The name Anegada is Spanish for the Drowned Land, which is a suited moniker for this island.

This is the northernmost island of the Virgin Islands and it has less 200 inhabitants. The area is completely surrounded by the barrier reef which makes sailing a lot more difficult. In fact, there are hundreds of ships that sunk off the coast, because the reef can only be seen when it's too late and the vessel gets caught. That is why most charter companies forbid sailing to this island. What is more, the local government forbade anchoring on the reef, in order to protect its ecosystem.

However, thanks to this incredible natural wonder, Anegada Island is a very popular area among divers and snorkelers. The reef is an actual maze with drops and tunnels, rich in many fish species including parrot fish and stingray. The hundreds of wreckages of

Spanish galleons, American and British ships will only enhance this incredible experience.

What is more, the island hoses many endangered species, from turtles, rock iguanas to flamingos. These colorful birds used to populate the island but they were hunted until extinction during the 19$^{th}$ and 20$^{th}$ century. In the past few decades, flamingos were reintroduced to the island, and visitor can admire these beautiful birds by the many large salt ponds spread over the western side of Anegada Island.

The deep waters by the northern tip of the islands are populated by hundreds of fish species, while domestic animals like donkeys, goats and sheep roam freely the green hills of the island.

Anegada Island is not only a destination for diver, but for beach lovers as well. There are several white sand beaches, many of them so large you'll find it difficult to encounter another person. The best ones are Bones Bight, Windlass Bight and Cow Wreck Beach. These stretches of sand are perfect for swimming thanks to the shallow calm waters protected by the barrier coral reefs.

# 9. Norman Island

Tourists with a penchant for pirate legends cannot miss the opportunity to explore Norman Island, on the southern part of the British Virgin Islands. This is one of several islands that are thought to have inspired Robert Louis Stevenson's famous pirate novel "Treasure Island".

Ever since the 19$^{th}$ century, many legends say that this island is the sight of many buried treasures. Norman Island is the largest uninhabited island in the British territory and one of the most popular for beach lovers.

The first writings about this island date back to the 18$^{th}$ century, when it is said that a Spanish galleon named Nuestra Senora de Guadalupe buried dozens of chests filled with silver coins on the beaches of Norman Island. Throughout the years, several locals from Tortola island and even a lieutenant general from Leeward Islands were able to discover parts of this treasure. But, legends of far greater wealth buried on the beautiful beaches of Norman Island still attract curious tourists even to this day.

The eastern side of the island, particularly the beaches at Benures Bay and Bight are among the only places that can easily be reached, the rest of the island is mostly untouched and very difficult to explore.

The area around the Bight feature three water level caves perfect for snorkeling. The caves are so remote and strange, that have fuelled the stories about great treasures hidden in these areas. These caves are also thought to have inspired Stevenson's book. One of the caves goes more than 70 feet underwater and divers gets the experience of night time diving during the day, since the sunlight barely penetrates the water.

In fact, Norman Island has a large number of hidden bays, caves and wrecks making this island a true playground for adventure loving tourists.

Courageous divers can try one of the best diving sites in the British territory. Less than a mile from the island, Santa Monica Rock features a diving pinnacle of almost 100 feet and is completely surrounded by deep waters. That is why divers can spot here larger fish including nurse sharks and spotted rays.

Though the island is uninhabited, there is a restaurant near Bight where visitors are welcomed with a hearty "Arrr!" great local dishes and delicious rum.

# 10. The Baths National Park

The most well-known spot on in the British Virgin Islands is the anchorage on the island of Virgin Gorda called the Baths. A little over a mile from the city of Spanish Town, on the southern area of the island, the Baths National Park boasts a unique geological formation. This bay is scattered with large granite boulders, many of which create grottoes and sea pools, perfect for snorkeling and diving. The boulders are as large as 40 feet in diameter.

There is a part of the beach where the boulders form a strange looking cave right on the beach. That actual spot is one of the most photographed places in the world, thanks to its distinctive features and interesting way the light reaches between these boulders.

Because of its unusual beauty, the area has become a major touristic attraction in the Caribbean and the local government declared the Baths a national park in 1990 in an effort to preserve de area intact.

Visitors can explore the surrounding using the rope handrails and steps which provide easy access to the more secluded areas. What is more, the Baths National Park also includes two other interesting areas: the Devil's Bay and the Spring Bay, which also has a great white sand beach perfect for sun bathing.

Though the landscape here is quite peculiar there's a simple explanation for the existence of these large boulders, some as big as a house. They are the result of molten rock seeping up into the already existing volcanic rock layers. Since this molten rock did not reach the surface, it cooled down slowly and it formed a hard crystalline granite layer. Throughout the centuries the rock shrunk and cracked and thus the blocks were formed while de round shape was given by the softer volcanic rock eroding away.

The Baths National Park is a great place for exploring and finding secluded coves and tunnels. Photographers will be thrilled to discover breathtaking landscapes hard to find anywhere else.

However, tourists in search for some down time in a more interesting surrounding can spend a few days here, on the beach swimming and sun bathing. Of course, snorkelers will have plenty of diving spots and great things to discover in the pools formed by these massive boulders.

If you are looking for an alternative way to spend time here, this entire area is quite striking from afar. Sailing into the deep blue waters will give you a brand new perspective over these amazing landscapes.

Copyright © 2015. All rights reserved.

Except as permitted under the United States Copyright Act of 1976, reproduction or utilization of this work in any form or by any electronic, mechanical, or other means, now known or hereafter invented, including xerography, photocopying, and recording, and in any information storage and retrieval system, is forbidden without written permission.

The ideas, concepts, and opinions expressed in this book are intended to be used for educational and reference purposes only. Author and publisher claim no responsibility to any person or entity for any liability, loss, or damage caused or alleged to be caused directly or indirectly as a result of the use, application, or interpretation of the material in this book.

Printed in Great Britain
by Amazon